7 Easy-to-Knit
HANDBAGS
for Every Occasion™

Jill Wright

Annie's®

A Note From the Designer

Handbags! We all carry our gear around in something, right? Every woman needs a tote to carry around her must-have, everyday things—glasses, lipstick, keys, mobile device, etc. I don't know about you, but I don't have time for juggling a handful of things I carry with me everywhere. I just grab my bag and head out the door. That's why handbags are so useful—they're ready to go at the drop of a hat!

We each have our own style, and as such we need a bag to fit with our needs. In this book you'll find seven very different styles for every occasion. Large or small, wide or narrow, zippered or buttoned, there's something here for all tastes, knit in a range of very affordable and readily available yarns.

Most of the designs are easy to make; a couple involve slightly more advanced techniques, but don't let that put you off. Each handbag has a very distinctive style—Luna is a big slouchy hobo-style bag with a boho attitude, and Dancette is a classy cable and intarsia clutch for the evening. But you also have patterns for everything in between. Now, let's go and knit some handbags!

Jill

Jill Wright

Table of Contents

....

Harriott,
page 4

Chastity,
page 24

Butternut,
page 14

Dancette,
page 11

Harriott

This large handbag has a zippered top and is worked in one long rectangle, which is then folded and sewn. The bag is held in shape with plastic canvas and has interior pockets and suede handles.

Skill Level
■■□□ EASY

Finished Measurements
5 inches x 14 inches x 9 inches

Materials
- Berroco Vintage (worsted weight; 50% acrylic/40% wool/10% nylon; 217 yds/100g per hank): 2 hanks each chocolate #5179 (A) and paprika #5157 (B)
- Size 4 (3.5mm) needles or size needed to obtain gauge
- 18-inch (1-inch-wide) zipper
- Thread to match zipper
- Sewing needle
- 3 sheets 10½ x 13½-inch plastic canvas
- 1 pair 24-inch-long suede handles

Gauge
23 sts and 44 rows = 4 inches/10cm in 2-Color Woven Pat.

To save time, take time to check gauge.

Pattern Stitch
2-Color Woven Pat (odd number of sts)
Row 1 (RS): With A, k1, *sl 1 wyif, k1; rep from * to end.
Row 2: Purl.
Row 3: With B, k2, *sl 1 wyif, k1; rep from * to last st, k1.
Row 4: Purl.
Rep Rows 1–4 for pat.

Handbag
With A, cast on 111 sts.

Work in 2-Color Woven Pat until piece measures 28 inches, ending with a Row 2.

With A, bind off.

Finishing
Weave in ends. Block.

Fold piece in half with WS tog (Fig 1). Sew side seams using mattress st (see page 28). Turn bag inside out, fold triangles at bag base so base measures 5 inches across; sew across base of triangles to form rectangular base of bag; sew tip of triangles to side seams (Fig 2). Turn RS out.

Cut 1 plastic canvas sheet to 5 inches deep for base. Sew one full plastic canvas sheet to each long side of base. Insert plastic canvas piece into bag with narrow section at base. Sew in place, leaving 2½ inches of bag free at top edge.

Pockets
Make 2

Using either color, cast on 36 sts.

Work 70 rows in St st.

Bind off.

Fold pocket in half and sew side seams. Sew one open edge to center top edge of plastic canvas. Sew 2nd pocket to other side.

Sew handles to bag approx 3 inches in from corners of bag and 3 inches down from top edge, sewing through both bag and plastic canvas for added strength.

Using needle and thread, sew in zipper (see page 28).

Fold down triangles at each end of top edge. Sew triangle tips to side seams. ●

FIG. 1

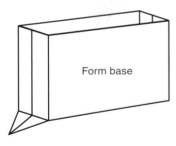

FIG. 2

Hobart

This is a firmer hobo-style bag worked sideways in a bulky yarn and a textured pattern stitch. A large decorative button closure and a purchased handle complete the look.

. . . .

Skill Level

■■□□ EASY

Finished Measurements
3 inches x 11 inches x 8 inches

Materials
- Kollage Yarns Lofty (bulky weight; 100% merino wool; 117 yds/100g per skein): 3 skeins mallard #8010
- Size 10 (6mm) needles or size needed to obtain gauge
- Size I/9 (5.5mm) crochet hook
- 1 (2¼-inch) button
- Thread to match button
- Sewing needle
- 1 (18-inch-long) handle

5 BULKY

Gauge
20 sts and 24 rows = 4 inches/10cm in Knot St pat.

To save time, take time to check gauge.

Pattern Stitch
Knot St (odd number of sts)
Rows 1 and 3 (RS): Knit.
Row 2: P1, *(p2tog, k2tog) in same 2 sts; rep from * across.
Row 4: *(P2tog, k2tog) in same 2 sts; rep from * to last st, p1.
Rep Rows 1–4 for pat.

Pattern Note
Bag is worked side-to-side, starting with gussets. Base is at center of body (as it is knit). Gussets are sewn to each other and to base to form sides.

Gusset

Cast on 41 sts.

Work 8 rows in Knot St pat; cut yarn then slide sts to other end of needle.

Make a 2nd piece in same manner, but do not cut yarn—2 gusset pieces on needle.

Joining row (RS): Work across 2nd piece, cast on 15 sts, work across first gusset piece—97 sts.

Work 3 rows even in established Knot St pat.

Body

Dec as follows:

Dec row (RS, dec): Ssk, knit to last 2 sts, k2tog—95 sts.

Work 7 rows even, maintaining Knot St pat.

Rep [last 8 rows] 6 more times—83 sts.

Inc as follows:

Work 2 rows even.

Inc row (RS): Kfb, knit to last st, kfb—85 sts.

Work 5 rows even, maintaining established Knot St pat.

Rep [last 8 rows] 6 more times—97 sts.

Gusset

Work across 41 sts, join 2nd ball of yarn and bind off 15 sts, work across 41 sts.

Working both sides at once with separate balls of yarn, work 7 rows even, maintaining established Knot St pat.

Bind off all sts.

Finishing

Note: If not familiar with chain (ch) and single crochet (sc) and slipped (sl) sts, refer to Crochet Class on page 29.

Fold in half with RS together. With WS facing and using back st, sew bound-off edges of gussets tog, then sew side edges of gussets to base (center body). Rep at other end.

Turn right-side out.

Beg at a top edge seam, crochet edging around top as follows: Ch 1; sc evenly around top edge, join with sl st to ch 1; cut yarn and fasten off.

Pockets
Make 2

Cast on 20 sts.

Work 20 rows in St st.

Bind off.

Turn bag inside out. Position a pocket centered on back and approx 1 inch from top edge of bag. Sew in place. Sew 2nd pocket in same position on front.

Handle Tabs
With RS facing, pick up and knit 9 sts across one gusset.

Row 1 (WS): P1, [k1, p1] 4 times.

Work even in established rib until tab measures 3 inches.

Bind off.

Rep on other side.

Attach Handles
Pass a tab through ring at end of strap, fold tab to inside of bag and sew in place.

Rep on other side.

Closure
Sew button approx 4 inches down from center top edge. Cut 3 strands of yarn 24 inches long. Use crochet hook to pull the strands through sc at top center of bag back. Fold strands in half, then divide into 3 groups of 2 strands. Work a 2-inch braid. Split strands into 2 groups of 3 strands, then braid each group for approx 2 inches. Use overhand knot to tie the braids tog; trim ends. Slip loop over button to close. ●

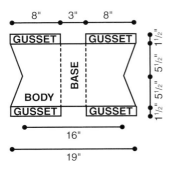

Dancette

Shimmery yarn adds style and elegance to this sleek clutch worked in intarsia cable panels.

. . . .

Skill Level

■■■▢ INTERMEDIATE

Finished Measurements
10 inches x 4½ inches

Materials
- S. Charles Collezione Stella (worsted weight; 74% silk/26% lurex; 76½ yds/ 25g per ball): 2 balls Milky Way #12 (A); 1 ball stormy skies #02 (B)
- Size 3 (3.25mm) needles or size needed to obtain gauge
- Cable needle
- 4 magnetic snaps
- Small piece of denim fabric (at least 8 square inches)

Gauge
30 sts and 44 rows = 4 inches/10cm in St st.

To save time, take time to check gauge.

Special Abbreviations
4 over 4 Left Cross (4/4 LC): Slip next 4 sts to cn and hold in front; k4, k4 from cn.

4 over 4 Right Cross (4/4 RC): Slip next 4 sts to cn and hold in back; k4, k4 from cn.

4 over 2 Left Purl Cross (4/2 LPC): Slip next 4 sts to cn and hold in front; p2, k4 from cn.

4 over 2 Right Purl Cross (4/2 RPC): Sl next 2 sts to cn and hold in back; k4, p2 from cn.

4 over 1 over 4 Right Purl Cross (4/1/4 RPC): Slip next 5 sts to cn and hold in back; k4, slip 5th st from cn to LH needle, p1, k4 from cn.

Make 1 purlwise (M1P): Insert LH needle from front to back under the running thread between the last st worked and next st on LH needle; purl into the back of resulting loop.

Pattern Stitches
Note: Charts are provided for those preferring to work pat sts from charts.

Horseshoe Cable (16-st panel)
Row 1 (RS): 4/4 RC, 4/4 LC.
Rows 2 and 4: P16.
Rows 3 and 5: K16.
Row 6: P16.
Rep Rows 1–6 for pat.

Diamond Cable (33-st panel)
Row 1 (RS): P12, 4/1/4 RPC, p12.
Row 2: K12, p4, k1, p4, k12.
Row 3: P10, 4/2 RPC, k1, 4/2 LPC, p10.
Row 4: K10, p5, k1, p1, k1, p5, k10.
Row 5: P8, 4/2 RPC, [p1, k1] twice, p1, 4/2 LPC, p8.
Row 6: K8, p4, [k1, p1] 4 times, k1, p4, k8.
Row 7: P6, 4/2 RPC, [k1, p1] 4 times, k1, 4/2 LPC, p6.
Row 8: K6, p5, [k1, p1] 5 times, k1, p5, k6.
Row 9: P4, 4/2 RPC, [p1, k1] 6 times, p1, 4/2 LPC, p4.
Row 10: K4, p4, [k1, p1] 8 times, k1, p4, k4.

Row 11: P4, 4/2 LPC, [k1, p1] 6 times, k1, 4/2 RPC, p4.
Row 12: Rep Row 8.
Row 13: P6, 4/2 LPC, [p1, k1] 4 times, p1, 4/2 RPC, p6.
Row 14: Rep Row 6.
Row 15: P8, 4/2 LPC, [k1, p1] twice, k1, 4/2 RPC, p8.
Row 16: Rep Row 4.
Row 17: P10, 4/2 LPC, p1, 4/2 RPC, p10.
Row 18: Rep Row 2.
Rep Rows 1–18 for pat.

Rope Cable (8-st panel)
Row 1: 4/4 RC.
Rows 2 and 4: P8.
Rows 3 and 5: K8.
Row 6: P8.
Rep Rows 1–6 for pat.

Pattern Notes
Bag worked flat in one piece.

The worsted-weight yarn is worked at a deliberately dense gauge to give the bag body.

Work the different-color panels with separate balls of yarn, using the intasia method. At color changes, twist the new color around the color just used.

Clutch
Cast on 16 sts B, 37 sts A, 4 sts B, 24 sts A—81 sts.

Work 6 rows in St st in established colors.

Eyelet row (RS): Maintaining colors, k8, k2tog, yo, k2, yo, k2tog, k14, k2tog, yo, k2, yo, k2tog, k13, k2tog, yo, k2, yo, k2tog, k14, k2tog, yo, k2, yo, k2tog, k8.

Work 4 rows in St st.

Inc row (WS): P8, [M1P, p1] 4 times, p20, [M1P, p1] 4 times, p1, [M1P, p1] 4 times, p28, [M1P, p1] 8 times, p8—99 sts.

Set-up row (RS): With A, k4, p4, work 16-st Horseshoe Cable, p4, k4; p4 B; with A, k4, work 33-st Diamond Cable, k4; with B, p4, work 8-st Rope Cable, p4, k4.

Work even in established pats until 6 reps of Diamond Cable are complete, then work Rows 1 and 2 of Diamond Cable panel.

Dec row (RS): K8, [k2tog] 8 times, k28, [k2tog] twice, k1, [k2tog] twice, k20, [k2tog] 4 times, k8—81 sts.

Work 5 rows in St st.

Eyelet row: K8, k2tog, yo, k2, yo, k2tog, k14, k2tog, yo, k2, yo, k2tog, k13, k2tog, yo, k2, yo, k2tog, k14, k2tog, yo, k2, yo, k2tog, k8.

Work 5 rows in St st.

Bind off.

Finishing
Fold piece in half; sew side seams.

Cut 8 (1-inch square) pieces of denim fabric. Cut 2 very short slits (approx ¼ inch) in each piece approx ½ inch apart.

Turn bag inside out, fold facings to WS, install magnetic snaps through eyelets using 1 denim square for each snap piece as stabilizer.

Sew facings to inside of clutch.

Weave in all ends. ●

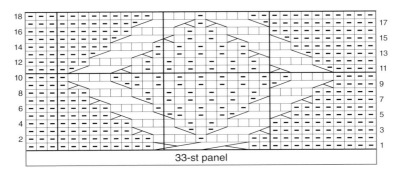

DIAMOND CABLE CHART

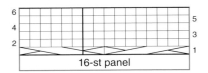

HORSESHOE CABLE CHART

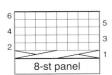

ROPE CABLE CHART

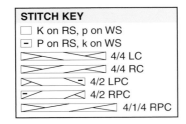

STITCH KEY
☐ K on RS, p on WS
⊟ P on RS, k on WS
4/4 LC
4/4 RC
4/2 LPC
4/2 RPC
4/1/4 RPC

Butternut

This potbelly bag begins with a 7-inch-square base, then grows into a ribbed body. The stockinette-stitch handles are secured to the handle tabs with large decorative knots.

Skill Level
◼◼◻◻ EASY

Finished Measurements
Base: 7 inches square
Circumference: Approx 30 inches (before being gathered)
Height: 10 inches

Materials
- Classic Elite Solstice (worsted weight; 70% organic cotton/30% wool; 100 yds/ 50g per hank): 2 hanks natural #2316 (A); 3 skeins Calais #2349 (B)
- Size 6 (4mm) straight and 24-inch circular needles or size needed to obtain gauge
- Size 8 (5mm) 24-inch circular needle or size needed to obtain gauge

Gauge
18 sts and 26 rnds = 4 inches/10cm in Wide Wale Rib pat with larger needle.

34 sts and 30 rows = 4 inches/10cm in Horizontal Herringbone pat with smaller needles.

To save time, take time to check gauge.

Pattern Stitches
Horizontal Herringbone (even number of sts)
Row 1 (RS): K1, *sl 1, k1, psso, but do not drop st from LH needle, knit into back of slipped st then drop both sts from needle tog; rep from * to last st, k1.
Row 2: *P2tog then purl first st again, slip both sts off needle tog; rep from * to end.
Rep Rows 1 and 2 for pat.

Wide Wale Rib
All rnds: *K5, p10, k5; rep from * around.

Special Technique
1-Row Buttonhole: Slip next 2 sts to RH needle; pass first st over 2nd st to bind off; [slip next st to RH needle, pass first st over 2nd st to bind off] twice; slip rem st back to LH needle; turn. Using cable method, cast 5 sts onto RH needle, turn; slip first st on LH needle to RH needle, then pass 1 cast-on st over the slipped st; continue working across row in stitch pattern.

Pattern Note
A square base is worked first. Body stitches are picked up around the base and worked in the round, then decreased at the top. The stitches are split in half to work the handle bases. The handles are worked separately, then threaded through button-holes and knotted in place.

Base
With A and smaller needles, cast on 58 sts.

Work in Horizontal Herringbone pat until base measures 7 inches.

Bind off.

Body
With B and smaller circular needle, beg at corner, pick up and knit 58 sts along each side of base; mark beg of rnd and join—232 sts.

Rnd 1: Knit around and inc 2 sts evenly across each side—240 sts.

Change to larger needle and Wide Wale Rib pat; work even until piece measures 8 inches from pick-up rnd.

Next rnd: *K3, k2tog, p2tog, p6, p2tog, ssk, k3; rep from * around—192 sts.

Next rnd: *K2, k2tog, p2tog, p4, p2tog, ssk, k2; rep from * around—144 sts.

Next rnd: *K1, k2tog, p2tog, p2, p2tog, ssk, k1; rep from * around—96 sts.

Work 2 rnds even, then k12; cut B.

Handle Tabs
Row 1 (RS): With smaller needle and A; work 48 sts in Horizontal Herringbone pat, turn, leaving rem 48 sts on hold on circular needle.

Work even for 1 inch, ending with a WS row.

Buttonhole row (RS): Work 3 sts, work 1-Row Buttonhole over next 4 sts, work to last 7 sts, work 1-Row Buttonhole over next 4 sts, work to end.

Work even until handle base measures 2 inches, ending with a WS row.

Bind-off row: [K2tog] twice, pass first st over 2nd st to bind off, *k2tog, pass first st over 2nd st; rep from * to end.

Rep on rem 48 sts.

Handles
Make 2

With smaller needles and A, cast on 10 sts.

Work in St st until piece measures 30 inches.

Bind off.

Finishing
Weave in all ends.

Thread ends of handles through buttonholes from inside to outside; knot ends to secure. ●

Ridgeway

This messenger-style handbag is worked in squares that are sewn together. The bag is closed with a button and finished with an over-the-shoulder knit strap.

· ·

Skill Level
 EASY

Finished Measurements
10 inches x 10 inches (not including 30-inch strap)

Materials
- Berroco Remix (worsted weight; 30% nylon/27% cotton/24% acrylic/ 10% silk/9% linen; 216 yds/100g per ball): 2 balls cocoa #3990
- Size 7 (4.5mm) needles or size needed to obtain gauge
- Size G/7 (4.25mm) crochet hook
- 1 (1½-inch-square) button
- Sewing needle
- Matching thread

Gauge
19 sts and 40 rows = 4 inches/10cm in Welt pat.

To save time, take time to check gauge.

Special Abbreviations
Make 1 (M1): Insert LH needle from front to back under the running thread between the last st worked and next st on LH needle; knit into the back of resulting loop.

Make 1 purlwise (M1P): Insert LH needle from front to back under the running thread between the last st worked and next st on LH needle; purl into the back of resulting loop.

Pattern Stitch
Welt
Rows 1–4: Work in St st.
Rows 5–8: Work in rev St st.
Rep Rows 1–8 for pat.

Pattern Note
Purse is composed of 4 welted squares and 1 welted triangle that are sewn together using cast-on and bind-off tails.

Square
Make 4

Increasing Half
Leaving a 24-inch tail, cast on 2 sts.

Row 1 (RS): K1, yo, k1—3 sts.

Rows 2 and 4: Purl.

Row 3: K1, M1, k1, M1, k1—5 sts.

Rows 5 and 7: P1, M1P, purl to last st, M1P, p1—9 sts.

Rows 6 and 8: Knit.

Continue in established Welt pat and inc 1 each end [every RS row] 21 more times, ending with Row 2 of pat—51 sts.

Decreasing Half
Row 1 (RS): Ssk, knit to last 2 sts, k2tog—49 sts.

Row 2: Purl.

Rows 3 and 5: Ssp, purl to last 2 sts, p2tog—45 sts.

Rows 4 and 6: Knit.

Row 7: Rep Row 1—43 sts.

Row 8: Purl.

Continue in established Welt pat and dec 1 st each end [every RS row] 20 more times, ending with a WS row—3 sts.

Next row: Ssk, k1—2 sts.

Bind off, leaving a 24-inch tail.

Triangle

Work Increasing Half.

Bind off.

Cut yarn, leaving a 24-inch tail.

Finishing

Block squares.

Using tails, sew squares tog with cast-on points in center and matching rev St st welts so that they form internal squares.

Fold 3 points of the square to center and sew tog to form front (4th point remains unsewn to form flap; see Fig 1). Sew triangle to angled sides of front to fill in the space.

Sew button approx 1 inch below center of front.

Button Loop

Note: If not familiar with chain (ch), refer to Crochet Class on page 29.

With RS facing, insert crochet hook into tip of flap and pull up loop of cast-on tail. Ch 7, insert hook into tip of flap, pull up loop, then fasten off. Weave in end.

Pockets
Make 2

Cast on 30 sts.

Work 40 rows in St st.

Bind off.

Turn bag inside out. Sew 1 pocket centered on inside front of bag and other to inside back, leaving top edges open.

Strap

With RS facing, pick up and knit 7 sts across one side edge of bag where front flap and front triangle meet.

Row 1 (WS): P1, [k1, p1] 3 times.

Work even in established rib until strap measures 30 inches.

Bind off, leaving a 12-inch tail.

Using tail, sew end of strap to opposite side of bag. ●

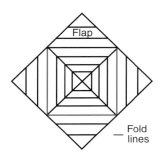

FIG. 1

Luna

A large hobo bag worked from the top down in two pieces with eyelet increases and broad shoulder strap will add style and color to your wardrobe. The interesting casual closure is a wrapped wooden bangle decorated with a selection of buttons. Braided ties finish the casual look.

Skill Level

■■■□ INTERMEDIATE

Finished Measurements
Approx 6 inches x 23 inches x 9½ inches (with 24-inch strap)

Materials
- Universal Yarn Classic Shades (worsted weight; 70% acrylic/ 30% wool; 197 yds/100g per skein): 4 skeins harvest #712
- Size 6 (4mm) needles or size needed to obtain gauge
- 1 (3¼-inch-diameter) bangle bracelet
- Assortment of buttons (sample used 15 buttons)

Gauge
24 sts and 40 rows = 4 inches/10cm in Welt pat.

To save time, take time to check gauge.

Pattern Stitch
Welt
Rows 1–6: Work in St st.
Rows 7 and 8: Work in rev St st.
Rep Rows 1–8 for pat.

Pattern Note
Front and back half-circles are worked the same, beginning at the center top edge, with increasing welt fabric radiating out to the outer edge, which is worked in stockinette stitch.

Handbag

Front
Cast on 11 sts.

Row 1: [K2, yo, pm, k1, yo] 3 times, k2—6 sts inc.

Rows 2, 4 and 6: Purl.

Rows 3 and 5: [Knit to marker, yo, slip marker, k1, yo] 3 times, knit to end—6 sts inc.

Row 7: Purl.

Row 8: Knit.

Rep [Rows 1–8] 10 more times, working Row 1 as for Row 3—209 sts.

Work 3 inches even in St st.

Bind off all sts.

Work back as for front.

Finishing
Block pieces.

Sew bound-off edges tog.

Strap
With RS facing, pick up and knit 21 sts across left top edge of back/front in final St st section.

Row 1 (WS): P1, [k1, p1] 10 times.

Work even in established rib until strap measures 24 inches.

Bind off all sts.

Sew bound-off edge to right top edge of front/back.

Button Ring
Leaving a 12-inch tail, wrap yarn tightly around bangle, ending where you began. Cut yarn, leaving a 36-inch tail. Tie tails tog.

String assorted buttons randomly onto longer tail; wrap buttoned-tail around ring, positioning buttons on one face of ring as you go. Tie tails tog again. Cut 1 more strand approx 16 inches long. Burying tail of new strand under yarn that's wrapped around bracelet, braid rem tails and new strand, leaving approx 4 inches unbraided. Thread braid through first and last eyelets of first row on back of bag; tie beg and end of braid tog using an overhand knot, forming a loop. Bury tails securely under wrapped yarns.

Weave in ends.

Ties
Cut 6 strands of yarn 36 inches long. Divide into 2 groups of 3 strands each. Thread first group through outer eyelet on first row of front of bag, fold in half, divide in 3 groups of 2 strands each. Braid yarns until approx 2 inches rem; knot ends and trim. Thread 2nd group of strands through opposite outer eyelet on first row of front of bag and braid in same manner. Tie in bow above button ring as closure. ●

Chastity

This simple tote is the perfect small shopping bag worked in intarsia color blocks with 1x1 rib handles.

. . . .

Skill Level

■ ■ ■ ▢ INTERMEDIATE

Finished Measurements
13 inches x 15 inches

Materials

- Brown Sheep Cotton Fleece (DK weight) 80% cotton/20% merino wool; 215 yds/ 100g per skein) 1 skein each wild sage #CW360 (A), cavern #CW005 (B), majestic orchid #CW915 (C) and putty #CW105 (D)
- Size 6 (4mm) needles or size needed to obtain gauge

Gauge
22 sts and 30 rows = 4 inches/10cm in St st.

To save time, take time to check gauge.

Pattern Notes
Bag is worked flat in one piece, then folded in half and seamed.

Color pattern is worked using the intarsia method. Use separate balls of yarn for each color section; at color changes, twist new color around color just used.

Bag
With D, cast on 75 sts.

Work in garter st until piece measures 1 inch, ending with a WS row.

Instarsia Pattern
*Row 1 (RS, set up intarsia pat): K15 C; with B, work 10 sts in k1, p1 rib; k50 A.

Maintaining C and A sections in St st and B section in rib, work even until piece measures 5 inches, ending with a WS row.

Next row (RS): Work C and B sections as established; k50 D.

Work 13 more rows, maintaining C and B sections as established and working D section in garter st; cut yarns, leaving 8-inch tails.

Next row (RS): K40 A; k35 B.

Work 13 more rows, working A section in St st and B section in garter st.

Next row: K40 A; with B, work 10 sts in k1, p1 rib; k25 C.

Maintaining A and C sections in St st and B section in rib, work even until piece measures 13 inches, ending with a WS row.

Next row (RS): K40 D, work to end in established pat.

Working D section in garter st and maintaining B and C section as established, work until piece measures 15 inches, ending with a WS row.

Rep [14-inch intarsia pat] once more.

Cut B and C, leaving 8-inch tails.

With D, work 1 inch in garter stitch.

Bind off.

Handles
Make 2

With D, cast on 7 sts.

Row 1 (RS): K1, [p1, k1] 3 times.

Work even in established rib until piece measures 22 inches.

Bind off.

Finishing
Fold piece in half and sew side seams.

Position handles 3 inches in from side seams with ends 2 inches down from top of bag. Sew in place.

Weave in all ends. ●

Knitting Basics

Long-Tail Cast-On

Leaving an end about an inch long for each stitch to be cast on, make a slip knot on the right needle.

Place the thumb and index finger of your left hand between the yarn ends with the long yarn end over your thumb, and the strand from the skein over your index finger. Close your other fingers over the strands to hold them against your palm. Spread your thumb and index fingers apart and draw the yarn into a "V."

Place the needle in front of the strand around your thumb and bring it underneath this strand. Carry the needle over and under the strand on your index finger.

Draw through loop on thumb.

Drop the loop from your thumb and draw up the strand to form a stitch on the needle.

Repeat until you have cast on the number of stitches indicated in the pattern. Remember to count the beginning slip knot as a stitch.

Backward-Loop Cast-On

This is the first cast-on that many knitters learn. It's very easy to do, but the first row is a little challenging to work. It's a handy one to use if you need to cast on stitches at the beginning or end of a row.

Step 1: Pick up the working yarn with your left hand to create a loop.

Step 2: Twist the loop around a half turn to the right, until it crosses over itself.

Step 3: Put the loop on the needle and pull the working yarn to tighten.

Cable Cast-On

This type of cast-on is used when adding stitches in the middle or at the end of a row.

Make a slip knot on the left needle. Knit a stitch in this knot and place it on the left needle. Insert the right needle between

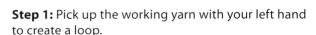

the last two stitches on the left needle. Knit a stitch and place it on the left needle. Repeat for each stitch needed.

Knit (K)

Insert tip of right needle from front to back in next stitch on left needle.

Wrap yarn under and over the tip of the right needle.

Pull yarn loop through the stitch with right needle point.

Slide the stitch off the left needle. The new stitch is on the right needle.

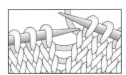

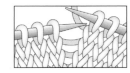

Purl (P)

With yarn in front, insert tip of right needle from back to front through next stitch on the left needle.

Wrap yarn around the right needle counter-clockwise. With right needle, draw yarn back through the stitch.

Slide the stitch off the left needle.

The new stitch is on the right needle.

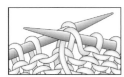
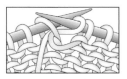

Invisible Increase (M1)

There are several ways to make or increase one stitch.

Make 1 With Left Twist (M1L)

Insert left needle from front to back under the horizontal loop between the last stitch worked and next stitch on left needle.

With right needle, knit into the back of this loop.

To make this increase on the purl side, insert left needle in same manner and purl into the back of the loop.

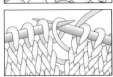

Make 1 With Right Twist (M1R)

Insert left needle from back to front under the horizontal loop between the last stitch worked and next stitch on left needle.

With right needle, knit into the front of this loop.

To make this increase on the purl side, insert left needle in same manner and purl into the front of the loop.

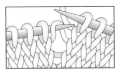

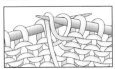

Increase (inc)

Two Stitches in One Stitch

Knit in Front & Back of Stitch (kfb)

Knit the next stitch in the usual manner, but don't remove the stitch from the left needle. Place right needle behind left needle and knit again into the back of the same stitch. Slip original stitch off left needle.

Purl in Front & Back of Stitch (pfb)

Purl the next stitch in the usual manner, but don't remove the stitch from the left needle. Place right needle behind left needle and purl again into the back of the same stitch. Slip original stitch off left needle.

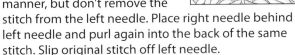

Decrease (Dec)

Knit 2 Together (K2tog)

Insert right needle through next two stitches on left needle as to knit. Knit these two stitches as one.

Purl 2 Together (P2tog)

Insert right needle through next two stitches on left needle as to purl. Purl these two stitches as one.

Slip, Slip, Knit (Ssk)

Slip next two stitches, one at a time, as to knit from left needle to right needle.

Insert left needle in front of both stitches and knit them together.

Slip, Slip, Purl (Ssp)

Slip next two stitches, one at a time, as to knit from left needle to right needle. Slip these stitches back onto left needle keeping them twisted. Purl these two stitches together through back loops.

Bind-Off

Binding Off (Knit)

Knit first two stitches on left needle. Insert tip of left needle into first stitch worked on right needle and pull it over the second stitch and completely off the needle.

Knit the next stitch and repeat. When one stitch remains on right needle, cut yarn and draw tail through last stitch to fasten off.

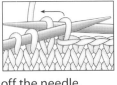

Binding Off (Purl)

Purl first two stitches on left needle. Insert tip of left needle into first stitch worked on right needle and pull it over the second stitch and completely off the needle.

Purl the next stitch and repeat. When one stitch remains on right needle, cut yarn and draw tail through last stitch to fasten off.

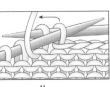

Zippers

It's simple to sew a zipper in by hand. This type of closure is used on the Harriott handbag on page 4.

Step 1: With the zipper closed and the public side of the garment pieces facing you, pin the zipper into place. Then, use contrasting sewing thread to baste the zipper into place with a running stitch.

Step 2: Remove the pins and whipstitch the zipper tape to the wrong side of the garment.

Step 3: With the public side of the fabric facing you, backstitch the zipper to the knitted fabric.

If there's any excess zipper tape at the top or bottom, fold it to the wrong side and tack it down. Remove basting thread.

Mattress Stitch

To work this seam, thread a tapestry needle with matching yarn. Insert the needle into one corner of work from back to front, just above the cast-on stitch, leaving a 3-inch tail. Take needle to edge of other piece and bring it from back to front at the corner of this piece.

Return to the first piece and insert the needle from the right to wrong side where the thread comes out of the piece. Slip the needle upward under the horizontal thread running between the first two stitches, and bring the needle through to the right side.

Cross to the other side and repeat the same process, going down where you came out, under two threads and up.

Continue working back and forth on the two pieces in the same manner for about an inch, then gently pull on the thread pulling the two pieces together.

Complete the seam and fasten off.

Use the beginning tail to even-up the lower edge by working a figure-8 between the cast-on stitches at the corners. Insert the threaded needle from front to back under both threads of the corner cast-on stitch on the edge opposite the tail, then into the same stitch on the first edge. Pull gently until the "8" fills the gap.

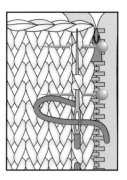
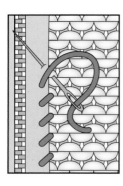
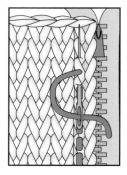

Knit Side   **Purl Side**

Pick Up & Knit

Step 1: With right side facing, working 1 st in from edge, insert tip of needle in space between first and second stitch.

Step 2: Wrap yarn around needle.

Step 3: Pull loop through to front.

Step 4: Repeat Steps 1–3.

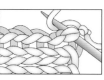

Backstitch

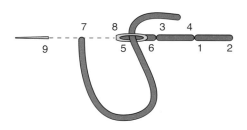

Cables in 3 Easy Steps

Cables are much easier to create than they appear. All you need is some yarn, a cable needle and the knitting needles of your choice.

There are just three easy steps for working a basic cable.

Step 1: Slide stitches onto a cable needle to hold them out of the way temporarily.

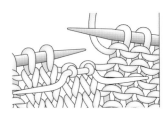

Step 2: Work the next stitches on the left-hand needle.

Step 3: Work the stitches from the cable needle.

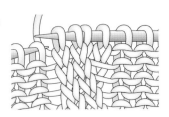

The pattern will always be specific as to how many stitches to slide onto the cable needle. It also will tell you whether the cable needle is to be held in front or in back of the work. This is very important because this is what causes the cable to twist to the left or to the right.

Intarsia

In certain patterns there are larger areas of color within the piece. Since this type of pattern requires a new color only for that section, it is not necessary to carry the yarn back and forth across the back. For this type of color change, a separate ball of yarn or bobbin is used for each section of color, making the yarn available only where needed.

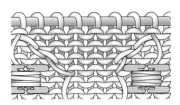

Purl Side

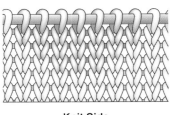

Knit Side

Before beginning the project, wind a bobbin for each color area, allowing ¾ inch for each stitch plus 10 inches extra to weave in at beginning and end of color section.

Bring the new yarn being used up and around the yarn just worked; this will twist, or "lock" the colors and prevent holes from occurring at the join. The top drawing shows how the two colors are twisted on the wrong side of the work and the bottom drawing shows what the pattern looks like from the front.

Crochet Stitches

Chain (ch)

Yarn over, pull through loop on hook.

Chain Stitch

Slip Stitch (sl st)

Insert hook under both loops of the stitch, bring yarn over the hook from back to front and draw it through the stitch and the loop on the hook.

Slip Stitch

Single Crochet (sc)

Insert the hook in the second chain through the center of the V. Bring the yarn over the hook from back to front.

Draw the yarn through the chain stitch and onto the hook.

Again bring yarn over the hook from back to front and draw it through both loops on hook.

For additional rows of single crochet, insert the hook under both loops of the previous stitch instead of through the center of the V as when working into the chain stitch.

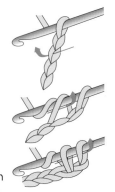

Single Crochet

Meet the Designer

Jill Wright has always loved knitting, from the ripe old age of 6 when her mom showed her the ropes. She learned how to crochet from a neighbor at age 8. Jill has been designing for many years but didn't start writing down her creations until recently. Jill had her first designs published in *Interweave Crochet* and *Crochet!* magazine in winter 2007 (both of them were handbags!).

Jill began having her knit designs published shortly afterward and has now had pieces published by *Creative Knitting* magazine, *Love of Knitting*, *Love of Crochet*, *Vogue Knitting International*, Bijou Basin Ranch, Zealana, Universal Yarn and Classic Elite Yarns.

Jill has co-authored a crochet booklet (*Curvy Crochet*) and has written a knitting book (*Taking The Fear Out Of Cables*), which is due to be published in 2013. Jill also teaches the *Lace & Openwork Knitting Workshop* online video class that is available through AnniesOnlineClasses.com, and she believes there is never enough time for working with yarn.

Resources

Berroco Inc.
1 Tupperware Drive, Suite 4
North Smithfield, RI
02896-6815
(401) 769-1212
www.berroco.com

Beverly Fabrics Inc.
9019 Soquel Drive
Aptos, CA 95003
(831) 728-2584
www.knitting-warehouse.com

Brown Sheep Co Inc.
100662 County Road 16
Mitchell, NE 69357
(800) 826-9136
www.brownsheep.com

Classic Elite Yarns
16 Esquire Road, Unit 2
North Billerica, MA 01862-2500
(800) 343-0308
www.classiceliteyarns.com

Kollage Yarns
3591 Cahaba Beach Road
Birmingham, AL 35242
(888) 829-7758
www.kollageyarns.com

Tahki Stacy Charles Inc.
70-60 83rd St. Bldg. #12
Glendale, NY 11385
(877) 412-7467
www.tahkistacycharles.com

Universal Yarn Inc.
5991 Caldwell Business Park Drive
Harrisburg, NC 28075
(704) 789-YARN (9276)
www.universalyarn.com

Many of the products found throughout this book are available at AnniesCatalog.com.

Photo Index

4

7

11

19

21

14

24

7 Easy-to-Knit Handbags for Every Occasion is published by Annie's, 306 East Parr Road, Berne, IN 46711. Printed in USA. Copyright © 2013 Annie's. All rights reserved. This publication may not be reproduced in part or in whole without written permission from the publisher.

RETAIL STORES: If you would like to carry this pattern book or any other Annie's publications, visit AnniesWSL.com.

Every effort has been made to ensure that the instructions in this pattern book are complete and accurate. We cannot, however, take responsibility for human error, typographical mistakes or variations in individual work. Please visit AnniesCustomerCare.com to check for pattern updates.

978-1-59635-686-3

1 2 3 4 5 6 7 8 9